C000132691

Written and illustrated by
Scoular Anderson

Contents

Introduction

Explorers are brave people who put their lives at risk
as they try to learn more about the world.

In this book, on the first page about each explorer
you will find a map of the world like this:

To find out where on earth each explorer went, use the map!
Follow the square *down* from the letter and *across* from
the number. Then turn over the page to find out more about
the explorers and their adventures.

Polynesians

Many thousands of years ago, people from South-east Asia began to make long journeys across the sea. They were some of the first explorers to make sea voyages of discovery. The places they found were often just specks of land scattered across the ocean.

Where on earth did they go?

Clue: go to G3.

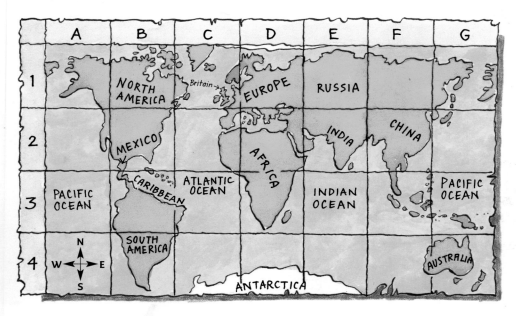

Answer: The Pacific Ocean

These sailors explored the Pacific Ocean without maps or equipment. Today, their **descendants** live on the Polynesian Islands, like Tonga, Tahiti and Hawaii or on larger islands like New Zealand.

The first sailors, like the Polynesians, had no maps or equipment to guide them.

They watched the pattern of clouds and waves.

They looked at the positions of the sun, moon and stars.

Seeing sea birds, seaweed and sea creatures often meant land was near.

Vikings

The Vikings came from northern Europe – from a place that's now called Scandinavia. They used their fast longships to travel great distances.

Most of them were **merchants** who traded things like furs and walrus tusks in exchange for jewellery and spices. Some of them were **raiders**. They attacked towns and farms and took away animals, or even people to sell as slaves.

Where on earth did they go?
Clue: go to B1 and C1.

Answer: North America and Britain

Two well-travelled Vikings were "Lucky" Leif Eriksson and Gudridur Thorbjarnardottir. Eriksson sailed across the Atlantic Ocean and built a house at a place he named Vinland.

Gudridur made the dangerous journey to Vinland. Her son was born there but her foster parents and her husband died on the journey.

That didn't put her off travelling. She decided to become a Christian and walked all the way to Rome to meet the Pope.

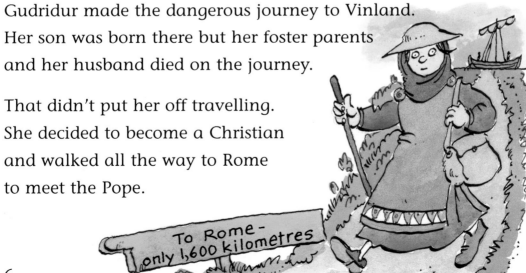

Marco Polo

Marco Polo's father and uncle were wealthy merchants from Venice who travelled far in search of luxury goods. In 1271 they set out on a journey along the Silk Road and took seventeen-year-old Marco with them. Marco didn't return home for another seventeen years.

Where on earth did they go?

Clue: go to F2.

Silk was carried along the Silk Road by camel caravans.

Turkey
To Europe
Syria
Iraq
Iran
India
The Silk Road
Tibet
China
Africa

Kublai Khan, the ruler of China, was very impressed by young Marco. He made him his **ambassador** and sent him around the country on business.

Marco wrote a book about his travels. Now many people don't believe he had been to China because he didn't mention some very common Chinese things in his book like...

chopsticks   Chinese writing
tea   the Great Wall of China

So was Marco Polo just a teller of tales?

Muhammad Ibn Batuta

Muhammad Ibn Batuta was born in Tangier on the north coast of Africa. In 1351 he set out on a long journey. On his travels he met several kings and saw great riches like camel caravans carrying packs of gold and salt. Salt was very valuable in those times.

Where on earth did he go?
Clue: go to F2.

Answer: China

During his adventurous life, Ibn Batuta visited more than forty countries and was even made ambassador to China by the Sultan of Delhi.

Unfortunately, he was attacked by bandits and lost all the treasure he was taking to China. He reached china eventually but only after being attacked by pirates, shipwrecked and marrying a princess!

On his last great journey, he travelled across the Sahara Desert to Timbuktu.

Tangier

Sahara Desert

Timbuktu

Christopher Columbus

In the **Middle Ages** most people thought
the world was flat, like a tray. They said that
if you sailed too far out to sea, you would
fall off the edge!

Christopher Columbus believed the world
was round, like an orange. In 1492 he set
out to prove this. He sailed west from Europe
and hoped to reach China. He never got
there, but he did get somewhere else!

Where on earth did he go?
Clue: go to B3.

Answer: The Caribbean

Columbus sailed across the Atlantic and arrived at an island in what is now called the Caribbean. This island was part of a land that was later named America.

The local people called themselves Caribs. Europeans named the place Caribbean.

Columbus took a month to cross the Atlantic.
During his life he made three more crossings and explored the Caribbean islands and the coast of South America.

Vasco da Gama

WANTED
A safe route for merchants in Europe to travel to the East to buy spices, silk and fine china. Anyone who can help should speak to the merchants as soon as possible.

A Portuguese sea captain called Vasco da Gama decided to try and find a safe **route** to the Far East by sea. He set sail in 1497 with three ships.

Where on earth did he go?

Clue: go to E2.

Answer: India

In the Middle Ages, merchants travelled overland to trade in places like India and China. The journey could take years and it was very dangerous.

Vasco da Gama discovered it was possible to sail round the southern point of Africa, the Cape of Good Hope. He had to put up with wild storms and riots from his crew but he found a local sailor who was willing to guide him to India.

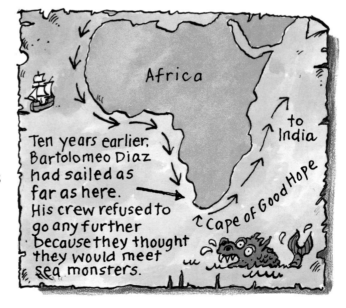

Ferdinand Magellan

In the Middle Ages, people from Europe loved to make their food tastier with spices. These came from the Spice Islands in the East.

Columbus had tried to find a route to the East by sailing west, but he found that North and South America blocked his way. Magellan was sure he could sail *round* America.

Where on earth did he go?

Clue: go to B4.

Answer: South America

Magellan's fleet of five ships was blown round the tip
of South America, Cape Horn, in a fierce storm.
They sailed into an ocean so calm that Magellan named
it *Pacifico* – which meant "peaceful" in Portuguese.

Only one ship and 24 sailors made it back home.
They were the first people to sail round the world.
Poor Magellan didn't get home as he was killed by
some Philippine islanders.

Francis Drake

Francis Drake was an English sea captain who made daring raids on Spanish lands and ships in South America. He made himself and his queen, Elizabeth I, very rich with the treasure he brought back. In 1577, the Queen sent him on a special **mission**.

Drake wasn't a pirate but a privateer. This meant he had a letter signed by the Queen saying that he had permission to attack enemy ships.

Where on earth did he go?
Clue: go to A3.

Answer: Pacific Ocean

Drake sailed round the tip of
South America (through the Straits
of Magellan) and up the west coast.
He attacked Spanish merchants' ships
as he went. He thought he might be
able to get home round the north coast
of North America but he couldn't find
a way through. Instead, he went across
the Pacific and became the first
Englishman to sail round the world.

Queen Elizabeth was so pleased with Drake, she came aboard his ship and **knighted** him.

The crowds who watched were so great that some people were pushed off the dock and into the smelly mud of the River Thames.

Hernan Cortez

Cortez was a Spaniard who lived on the Caribbean island of Cuba. He heard people talk about the fabulous gold to be found in a land to the west. He sold his farm to buy some ships, then set out on a voyage of discovery.

Where on earth did he go?
Clue: go to B2.

Answer: Mexico

Cortez and his men landed in Mexico in 1519.
They became known as *Conquistadors* (conquerors).
They attacked the local people – the Aztecs – and took
over their lands. Cortez surrounded the magnificent
capital city of the Aztecs. The Aztecs were defeated
in battle because they didn't have
swords and guns like the Spanish.

> The Aztecs had never seen horses
> so the sight of Spanish soldiers
> sitting on them was terrifying.

Besides gold, the Spanish brought other things
from Mexico.

sweet peppers

potatoes

tomatoes

maize

turkeys

James Cook

In 1768, Captain Cook was sent from England to the far side of the world with some scientists who wanted to study the planet Venus. While he was there he tried to find the "unknown land" which other sailors had talked about.

Where on earth did he go?
Clue: go to G4.

Cook's first ship was the Endeavour. It was a cargo ship more used to carrying coal. It was chosen for its sturdiness.

Answer: Australia

Cook found the "unknown land". Today it's called Australia. He drew **accurate** maps of its coast, sailed round New Zealand and even reached the icebergs of Antarctica.

In those days, many sailors died of a disease called scurvy which was caused by bad diet. Cook's crew stayed healthy because he whipped anyone who didn't eat their **ration** of pickled cabbage and limes, which prevented the disease.

The signs of scurvy
Sleepiness
Dry hair
Bad breath
Teeth fall out
Aching joints

On his third voyage, Cook began to suffer from a stomach illness which made him very bad-tempered. This could be why he got into an argument with some Hawaiians over a stolen boat. The Hawaiians killed Cook.

David Livingstone

David Livingstone, the Scottish explorer, was almost eaten by a lion – and cannibals! As he crossed deserts and trekked through jungles and swamps, he grew weak with disease but still kept going.

Livingstone's wife travelled with him for a while, until he persuaded her to go home with their children.

Where on earth did he go?
Clue: go to D3.

Answer: Africa

Livingstone went to Africa in 1840 to **convert** the local people to Christianity. He didn't have much success with this, so he decided to explore instead. He travelled up and down all the main rivers in a steam boat. He was the first European to travel from the west coast to the east coast of Southern Africa.

Livingstone disappeared for six years. Everyone thought he was dead. A journalist and explorer called Henry Stanley was sent to find him. After searching for a year, he found Livingstone alive.

Doctor Livingstone, I presume.

Samuel and Florence Baker

Samuel Baker and his wife Florence travelled up
the longest river in the world. No one knew where
the river began and they wanted to find out.

Where on earth did they go?

Clue: go to D2.

Answer: Africa

The Bakers travelled up the
River Nile. They got to Gondoroko
where no European had been –
or so they thought. There, they
met John Speke and James Grant
who had found that the Nile
flowed from a great lake.

There's another branch of
the Nile still to explore.

After a dangerous journey, the Bakers found
another place where the Nile flowed from.

Florence kept a diary and made maps
of their journey. Queen Victoria was shocked
to hear that Florence had worn *trousers*
while in Africa!

Roald Amundsen and Robert Scott

In 1910, Robert Scott set sail from Cardiff on the ship *Terra Nova*. He was trying to get to one of the few places on the planet still to be explored and he wanted to be the first man to reach its centre.

When he heard that a Norwegian called Roald Amundsen had had exactly the same idea, the journey became a race.

Where on earth did they go?

Clue: go to D4.

Answer: Antarctica

Both men arrived in Antarctica at the end of 1911 and both men wanted to be first to reach the South Pole.

Amundsen set up base at the Bay of Whales, 96km nearer to the Pole than Scott.

Antarctica
South Pole

Mountains
Glacier

Scott set up base at McMurdo Sound.

When Scott eventually arrived at the South Pole, he found Amundsen's flag already there. He had lost the race. On the return journey, Scott and his men died of the terrible cold – just 18 kilometres from his **depot** of supplies.

Scott was not as prepared for the extreme weather conditions as Amundsen.

Scott and his men wore cotton and woollen clothes. These became soaked with sweat which then turned wet and cold.

Scott's men had to pull their sleds after the ponies they brought died of cold.

Amundsen's team wore furs which were warm and let their bodies breathe naturally.

They used skis and sleds pulled by **Huskies** which were used to the cold.

Glossary

accurate	without a mistake
ambassador	the representative of a country
convert	to change someone or something
depot	a store
descendants	people living now who are related to people in the past
Huskies	Arctic dogs
knighted	to be made a knight
merchants	people who buy and sell goods
Middle Ages	the years between 1000 and 1499
mission	a task
raiders	attackers
ration	a fixed amount of food
route	the way to a place

Where did they go?

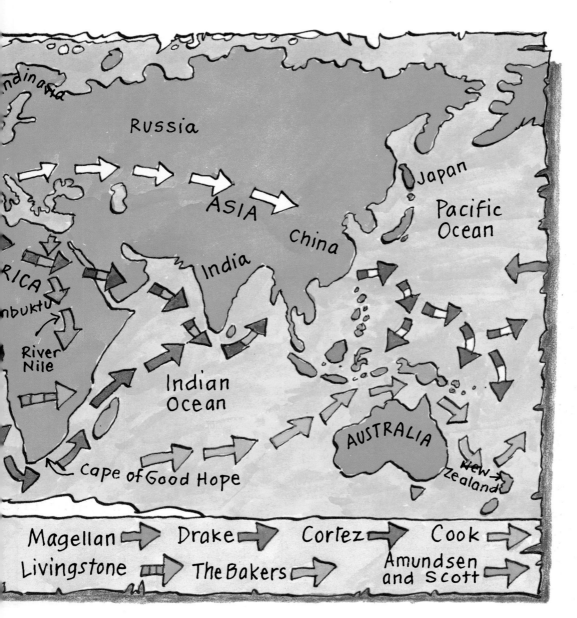

Ideas for guided reading

Learning objectives: locate information using contents, headings, sub headings, etc; to infer the meaning of unknown words from context; present events and characters through dialogue to engage the interest of an audience.

Curriculum links: Geography – Where in the World is Barnaby Bear?; Passport to the World.

Interest words: Polynesians, descendants, Vikings, Scandinavia, Leif Eriksson, Gudridur Thorbjarnardottir, Marco Polo, Kublai Khan, Muhammad Ibn Batuta, Sahara desert, ambassador, Christopher Columbus, Atlantic, Vasco da Gama, Ferdinand Magellan, Francis Drake, Hernan Cortez, Caribbean, conquistadors, James Cook, David Livingstone, Samuel and Florence Baker, Roald Amundsen and Robert Scott

Word count: 1,582

Resources: globe

Getting started

This book can be read over two guided reading sessions.

- Discuss facts the children already know about explorers. Prompt using names such as Christopher Columbus.

- Using the globe, remind children of the locations of the continents and oceans. Discuss routes for travelling from Europe right around the world.

- Look at the contents page and spot names already known to pupils – which names do they think might be from other countries and why? (Stress use of unusual spellings.)

- Explain how to use the grid maps and model the first example on p3. Ask the children to try using the grid on p5 themselves.

Reading and responding

- Ask the children to read quietly and independently to p19. Then ask them to scan through what they have read again, and try to remember new facts, as you will be quizzing them shortly. Praise children for skimming and scanning for information.